VOCAL SELECTIONS

Taking my Turn.

Vocal Score. Selections

Lyrics by WILL HOLT   Music by GARY WILLIAM FRIEDMAN

"...a musical about aging that is irrepressibly young at heart."

New York Times, 6/10/83

Background story-biographical data, see back cover

Original Cast album: Broadway Entertainment Records BLR-1001-R

Road companies: Florida; United States bus and truck tour - summer 1984; international companies in Germany, Holland, Japan and South Africa

Television productions: "Great Performers Series," PBS telecast, 1985; "Prime of Your Life" theme song (This Is My Song), NBC weekly show

Featured entertainment: 25th Anniversary Convention AARP (American Association of Retired Persons), April 1984, St. Louis

TRO **HAMPSHIRE HOUSE PUBLISHING CORP. / DEVON MUSIC, INC.**
in association with
LEMON TREE MUSIC, INC. and BUSSY MUSIC.

MB598   452

From the Musical Production "TAKING MY TURN"

THIS IS MY SONG

Lyric by
WILL HOLT

Music by
GARY WILLIAM FRIEDMAN

Once a-gain to feel the thrill___ of A-pril ris-ing on the hill.___
Soon e-nough we feel the chill___ of Au-tumn ris-ing on the hill.___

Once a-gain to know the pain___ and taste the joys___ of love a-gain.___
Soon e-nough we know we might___ not quite re-cov-er from the night.___

5

From the Musical Production "TAKING MY TURN"

FINE FOR THE SHAPE I'M IN

Lyric by
WILL HOLT

Music by
GARY WILLIAM FRIEDMAN

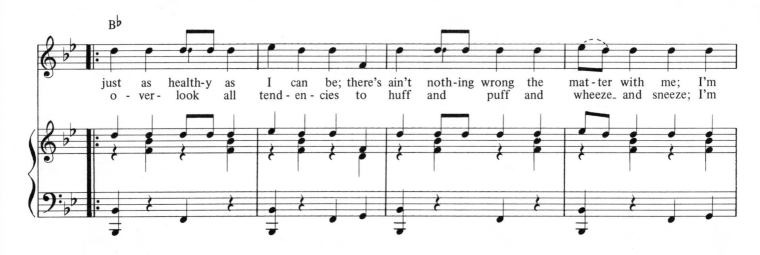

just as health-y as I can be; there's ain't noth-ing wrong the mat-ter with me; I'm
o-ver-look all tend-en-cies to huff and puff and wheeze and sneeze; I'm

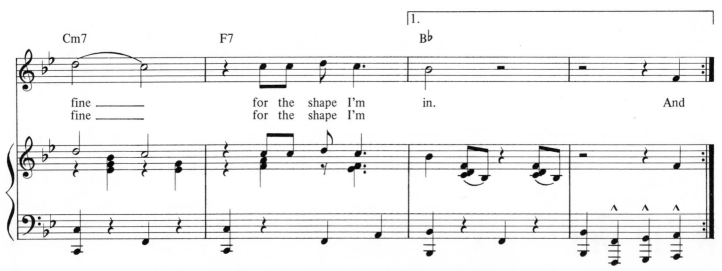

fine _____ for the shape I'm in. And
fine _____ for the shape I'm

2.

B♭

in.

E♭

O there are aches and there is pain and I
Arch sup - ports sup - port my feet; it

Gm

C7

al - ways know when it's gon - na rain 'cause my el - bow acts like a
takes me hours to cross the street; I can't stand cold and I

F7sus4   **F7**   **B♭**

weath - er vane but I don't com - plain. For the one thing no one
can't get heat but I still re - peat. I may be liv-ing on

wants to know___ when they say, "How are___ ya?" and mean___ "Hel - lo"___ is
as - pi - rin___ but I make damn sure___ I say with a grin___ I'm

From the Musical Production "TAKING MY TURN"

TWO OF ME

Lyric by
WILL HOLT

Music by
GARY WILLIAM FRIEDMAN

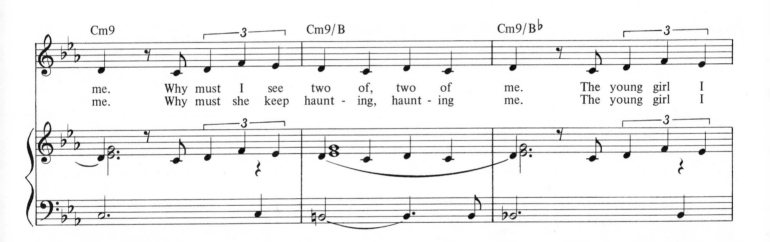

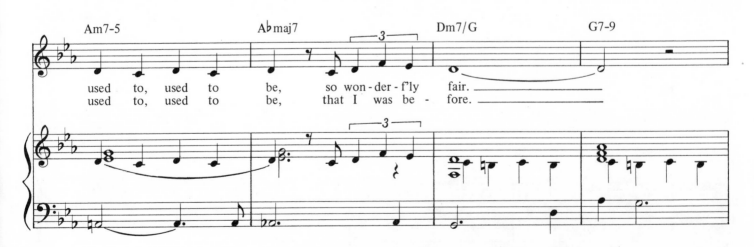

From the Musical Production "TAKING MY TURN"

PICK MORE DAISIES

Lyric by
WILL HOLT

Music by
GARY WILLIAM FRIEDMAN

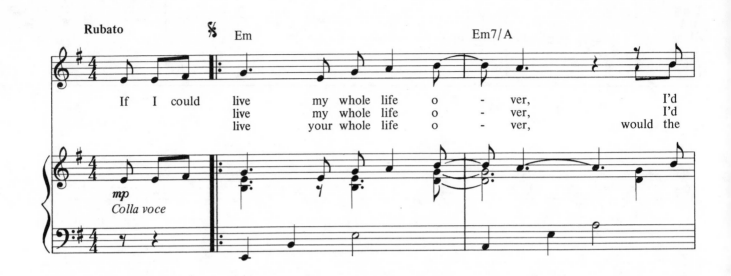

Rubato

Em   Em7/A

If I could live my whole life o - ver,   I'd
live my whole life o - ver,   I'd
live your whole life o - ver,   would the

mp
Colla voce

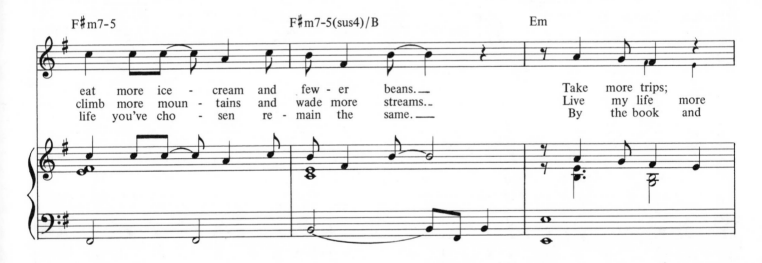

F♯m7-5   F♯m7-5(sus4)/B   Em

eat more ice - cream and few - er beans.___   Take more trips;
climb more moun - tains and wade more streams.___   Live my life more
life you've cho - sen re - main the same.___   By the book and

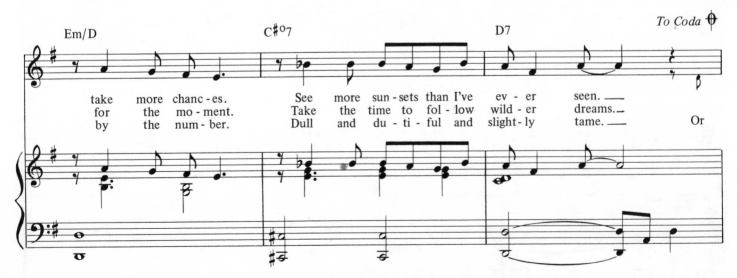

Em/D   C♯°7   D7   *To Coda* ⊕

take more chanc - es.   See more sun - sets than I've ev - er seen.___
for the mo - ment.   Take the time to fol - low wild - er dreams.___
by the num - ber.   Dull and du - ti - ful and slight - ly tame.___ Or

From the Musical Production "TAKING MY TURN"

TAKING MY TURN

Lyric by
WILL HOLT

Music by
GARY WILLIAM FRIEDMAN

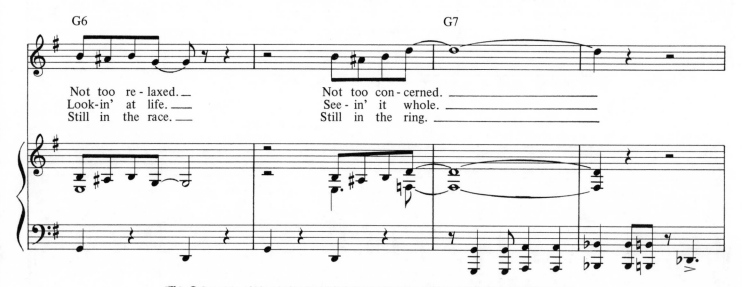

CODA

From the Musical Production "TAKING MY TURN"

I AM NOT OLD
(He Strengthens Me So)

Lyric by
WILL HOLT

Music by
GARY WILLIAM FRIEDMAN

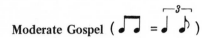

Moderate Gospel

I am not old! _____ Though peo-ple say _____
I am not old! _____ Though sight grows dim _____

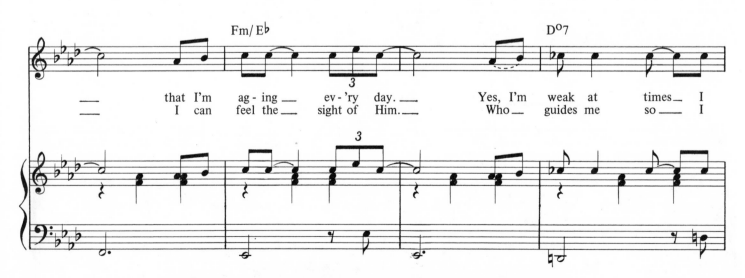

that I'm ag-ing ev-'ry day. _____ Yes, I'm weak at times I
I can feel the sight of Him. _____ Who guides me so I

23

From the Musical Production "TAKING MY TURN"

GOOD LUCK TO YOU

Lyric by
WILL HOLT

Music by
GARY WILLIAM FRIEDMAN

From the Musical Production "TAKING MY TURN"

IT STILL ISN'T OVER

Lyric by
WILL HOLT

Music by
GARY WILLIAM FRIEDMAN